WHAT ARE YOU LOOKING FOR?

WHAT ARE YOU LOOKING FOR?

Seeking the God Who Is Seeking You

Joan Chittister, OSB

Paulist Press
New York / Mahwah, NJ

Cover image by Meranna/Shutterstock.com. Author photo by Ed Bernik. Cover and book design by Lynn Else

Library of Congress Control Number: 2018963232

ISBN 978-0-8091-5474-6 (paperback)
ISBN 978-1-58768-788-4 (e-book)

Published by Paulist Press
997 Macarthur Boulevard
Mahwah, New Jersey 07430
www.paulistpress.com

Printed and bound in the
United States of America

Contents

Chapter 1

WHY WOULD I WANT TO TALK TO ANYONE ABOUT RELIGIOUS LIFE?

"A single conversation across the table with
[the] wise...is better than ten years'
mere study of books."

Henry Wadsworth Longfellow

It's important that we meet, you and I. So, unlikely as it may seem that the two of us would be able to connect under ordinary conditions, I'm asking you to continue reading now. Why? Because before you chart your own future directions in life, you need to think again about a life option that has been important to hundreds of thousands of people in the past. You need to talk to someone about one of life's major choices that has recently changed greatly but whose older stereotypes still linger. Most of all, you need to consider the meaning of it all with someone who has been on both sides of this ancient but always evolving institution. Religious life is a subject that has had phenomenal influence in the past and has made all of its present changes for the sake of helping to do the same in our own very fluid present as well.

1

WHAT ARE YOU LOOKING FOR?

So, this book poses a very big question. It describes a singular choice—one dedicated to a life lived entirely through the filter of the gospel. But this conversation is not just for people who might be thinking of pursuing some kind of religious commitment themselves. It's for all people who care about the place and nature of religious life in the Christian community as much as you do. After all, it has shaped generation after generation of the Church. We all need to think again about what it is. About what it's attempting to do. About what it's become in the last fifty years. About what value it has to anybody—whether they want to be a part of it or not.

It's also certainly for people who may actually be at the point of deciding whether they themselves ought to enter a religious community now. In this day and age. In this society. Some readers will have had years in public life but find themselves looking for more out of life. As in, "Is that all there is?" Many will be younger and only beginning to explore the multiple opportunities the world seems to offer. It's important that they consider them all.

Others may feel, however much the world seems to offer them, that such a life is simply not profound enough for them to spend a life on.

Whatever life's present circumstances, good as they may be, many will feel that something is still missing in life, at least for them.

Questions like these cannot be taken lightly. These concerns, these issues, need a lot of good information, a lot of serious thought. Those seeking answers need the opportunity to talk to someone who has been there, who has lived a religious life, who can answer some very important but very difficult questions. That's why I'm here. I've been in religious life for years. I know what it's about. I know the big questions. I have had the time, then, to live into some answers—at least for me.

You have every right to wonder what I can possibly tell you, of course. After all, I am in my eighties now. You, in contrast, are young—years younger than that, for sure. You have a lot of life ahead of you yet. That's why it's doubly important that you think through those years and those options. Decisions like this one that have the power to affect your whole life deserve a special kind of consideration, one that is based more on human values than on career advancement. It is a precious and sacred decision you are about to make. It's definitely too sacred a moment in life to be cavalier about. You must make your choices consciously, pour them out wisely, strew them across the years lovingly.

The very idea of a vocation to religious life is overwhelming: You, whoever you are, are on the verge of change. Like the fishermen Jesus found on the beach in Israel and invited to follow him, the very thought of becoming a disciple is a daunting one. After all, when there is no reason to change, why change?

You have a life to spend, a world to find, a contribution to make, the very depths of the self to penetrate. More, the choices you make about your future will affect others as well. How do I know that? For two reasons: First, because that's what life is about. Purpose is the core of it and reckless generosity is its gold standard. Without both those things, life dulls or sours or simply drones on endlessly. There is no happiness or sense of fulfillment in the eternal drift toward meaninglessness. If any life is to have meaning, a direction must be found.

The very thought of going through life like a leaf on the wind, wondering how you got here and where you might end up before it's over is, at best, sad. Every day is a day meant for living life to the full. We aren't here to waste life, we're here to shape it. To make something out of it that makes life better for the rest of the world, as well as for ourselves.

But second, you wouldn't be reading this book if you didn't know the truth of that, at least subconsciously. If you weren't already looking for something special on which to inscribe the best of yourself, you would not have even read this far. Which is why I think a conversation between generations on a subject like this is important. There are so many differences to consider between the kinds of choices people made years ago and the ones they make today. But more important than those differences is the fact that there are also so many similarities to explore in this universal and eternal quest for the meaning of life. That's why you and I have a lot to talk about. What's really important in life? What things last in life—like meaning and happiness—and what things don't—like money and status, perhaps.

The problem, of course, is precisely that: I am old and you are not. You are "modern," they say, and I am not. The assumption, of course, is that *modern* is a synonym for "different." But that's not true. We are all the same at the center of ourselves, where the heart and the soul come together. Bodies grow old; hearts and souls do not. They stay forever young, forever searching from day to day for the juice of it. For the electricity that makes life worthwhile. So, let's say it this way: you are fewer in years than I am, yes, but, at one level, we are both young, both forever searching for a life that is inestimable, is important, is about more than personal advancement.

That is exactly why you and I need to talk through these things together for a while.

But let's be clear: We do not need a conversation about "the good old days," about what religious life was when I entered, for instance. We need to talk about what you can expect of it in days to come. If religious life is to continue to be a witness to the will of God for the next two thousand years as it has been for the last two thousand years, we must ask what we should be able to find there still. After all, early Christian communities, just like us, were devoted to spreading the word that makes life better for everyone everywhere. They gave their lives, literally, and without reserve. And to do it they lived in communities many saw as useless, baseless, and meaningless. And yet it was those communities that became the social system of Europe, that settled the New World, and that brought generation after generation of new Americans to a new level of life.

Why Would I Want to Talk to Anyone about Religious Life?

We are all, lay and religious together, on our way home to the God who made us. Finding the path that fits us so that we may thrive on it and it may be better because we have been there is the purpose of life. There is in every heart, therefore, a magnet for good to guide us on the way.

The truth is that I have no interest in the "good old days" either. I am more concerned about what I have learned about the universal underpinnings of religious life in the more than sixty years that I have lived it. It's those things I want you to look for: Not period costumes or a significant place or even particular works in a false hierarchy of vocations. There is only one vocation in life and that is to seek the God who is seeking us. And that one we all have.

It is the basic elements of a life lived in the shadow of Jesus that religious life is really all about. It's those things that are important, no matter which era of religious life we're talking about. These are the things that make religious life a way of life rather than simply another kind of institutional service. Good works come and go; they change from era to era, depending on the needs of the world in every age. But what does not change in religious life is the ongoing growth into the mind of God that religious life develops in us as we go on in it from age to age.

It's that which the young of every generation are intent on discovering but have yet to define. It is also that which older women and men religious have already tasted and so ought to be able to be counted on to be honest about.

I named this book *What Are You Looking For?* The title is not original. It comes right out of the Gospel of John as one apostle after another struggles with whether or not Jesus's invitation to total discipleship, on living the spiritual life as he lived it, is meant for them. It's not a sales talk he gives them. It's not a proposition: a bargain that promises this for that. It's not a reward-loss model. It is the invitation to a lifelong relationship with God, unique for its totality, precious for its particular kind of intimacy. It's not about being able to demonstrate a particular educational skill or achieve a particular ambition. It is about much more than that. It is about wholeheartedness, about the giving of the self without reserve for the sake of a purpose larger than the self.

It is about immersing oneself in the mind of God so that the world can also see the presence of Jesus in us.

But what exactly does that mean? What does it mean to you? What will you mean to the world as a result of it?

Those answers depend on your staying in the conversation.

"And Jesus said to them, 'Follow me and I will make you fish for people'" *(Mark 1:17).*

Chapter 2

ISN'T RELIGIOUS LIFE BECOMING EXTINCT NOW?

> "He [or she] who refuses to learn
> deserves extinction."
>
> *Rabbi Hillel*

I was taken off guard a bit by the question with which she began the conversation. "I really admire people who commit themselves to religious life," she said. "But how do you know that it isn't already extinct?"

I was sitting with someone who has been in a kind of undefined relationship with a religious community for months. Maybe years, if truth were known. She was the epitome of those almost-but-not-quite members that are so common in this interim period between the past and the future of institutional religious life.

Anyone who has ever been fascinated by a possibility but shy about pursuing it knows the feeling of it. We circle an idea, a place, an intriguing possibility for years before we finally give in to the lure of it. It can take a good deal of reflection before we finally admit to ourselves that in this idea or place or—harder yet—in this commitment lies the central concern of our life.

7

WHAT ARE YOU LOOKING FOR?

We finally acknowledge to ourselves, however, that until we resolve the questions this attraction poses for us, we cannot really be sure of anything else in life. Either that or we will continue to be haunted by it years later. We become the kind of person who says, "Well, I thought about it quite seriously but I never did anything about it....So life just went on."

Indeed, life goes on. But to where?

Answer: too often to nowhere. To nothing I felt was quite right for me. To nothing that said "fullness of life" to me ever. When we don't decide before we take a major step in life what we want out of life as a result of it, regret is more likely to become an invisible but palpable companion. It's that moment on the high diving board that we never quite manage to forget. It's the one where you climb the ladder, look into the water below, and back off the board without ever discovering if it just might be in that water where you could have found the real you.

The woman went on talking about our extinction. But she also made it clear that she herself wanted to live a life of total self-giving to the world around her. I smiled a bit as I remembered another conversation in another place. "Sister," the man in the audience remarked, "if you all eliminate the religious habit, you are going to lose all respect." And then he went on, "If you don't have schools anymore, where are new members going to come from?"

I thought for a moment and then decided that only honesty could begin to answer such a question as this. I could talk about the mystery of "call," of course. Or maybe the story of Jesus picking the apostles would help. Or the now theologically discredited promise of reward that went with having a "higher vocation" might do it. But all of those ideas were patently superficial. So, instead, I said, "Well, I really don't know. Where do gynecologists get new gynecologists? Gynecologists don't have grade schools. Or where do astronauts find new astronauts to succeed them? As far as I know, they don't recruit them as children. So, are we running out of them?" I said. And then it dawned.

Isn't Religious Life Becoming Extinct Now?

The truth is that we are all born with distinguishing gifts toward one kind of life or another: We bear within ourselves natural tendencies to the light or the dark dimensions of service, to private or public involvements, to speculative or activist ways of being in the world, to the contemplative or active spiritual life. And it is to those things we orient our lives. It's in those places that our souls are at home.

Viability in religious life is not a numbers game. Otherwise, we need to ask the same question of marriage: Is marriage becoming extinct simply because, at least in our era, it seems to be less stable or more fragile than we expected it to be before divorce became an option? More than 40 percent of first marriages, they tell us, end in divorce now. Isn't it really just as true to say that our long, long lives have made serial monogamy more common than the lifelong marital commitments of shorter-lived people of earlier generations?

No, in a period of great social change like our own, when more and different options are suddenly emerging, the catalogue of human possibilities has expanded. In fact, it is precisely in such a period as now that we need to explore the depths of the self before we make great life decisions. It is within us—not in the nature of the institutions around us—that commitment lies. Institutions change as society changes. But that kind of change does not necessarily change the depth or stability of the initial commitment itself.

Married life changed as women began to work outside the home, but marriages remained intact. Gendered roles changed as men, too, became nurses and elementary school teachers and women chose to specialize in computer science rather than nursing. But those educational choices did not change what it meant to be a woman or a man.

And so it is with religious commitment. Religious commitment will become what committed religious say it must be if it is to retain its true identity and purpose. And that could well change in form but not in spirit from era to era as it has for centuries.

WHAT ARE YOU LOOKING FOR?

What does not change is the essence of the vocation to holiness itself. Married couples will live it one way. Single people will live it another. Committed religious will remain a third kind of sign of the Christian community on pilgrimage. They will move before us and among us holding up the flag of lifelong commitment to the spiritual life so that we all remember our own call to commitment, whatever the path we've chosen.

And do I myself know the truth of it? Indeed, I do. A council of the Church was calling the Church to change. Static for years, the Church of the twentieth century looked and acted more like the nineteenth. Already on the cusp of the twenty-first century, the early religious life seemed to have come to a standstill. Until it erupted, that is.

Suddenly, change was everywhere: the clothes we wore changed, the works we did, the way we now went through life alone, as adult women, rather than with companions—common for women in the Victorian era. Even the way we lived together, said our prayers together, did our work together was evolving.

It was an exciting time, but it was a fearful time as well. We ourselves began to ask the question, first secretly, then aloud: Was religious life dying right under our feet as we walked to new places, met new people, took on new challenges like nuclear disarmament, the oppression of women, even the renewal of the liturgical prayers monasteries had been saying for generations?

The polarization of the period was wearying. It weighed us down and left us feeling "too old to leave religious life, too young to stay." And in fact, many of us did leave under the burden of the confusion. Or some simply began to realize that this life was not really their life at all. They learned that whatever earlier generations believed about the moral permanency of religious vows, that they could only be faithful to the God within them if they left this lifestyle for another.

And yet, little by little, a new light dimmed in the darkness of it all and we began to see the very purpose of the time: Like the Israelites who had wandered in the desert for forty years as they moved from Egypt to the promised land, so were we, as God's people, in process as well. And not only us but the whole Church, the whole world. If anything would promise its extinction, it was surely a lack of faith, not trust in the future. We were all, together, taking another step on the road to the will of God for this changing time and place and people. We discovered that we were in religious life to be faithful, not permanent. We were actually meant to be communities of change, to learn the needs of the time, to be communities faithful to the ongoing and unending quest for God in this changing time and place.

Religion and religious life is not immune to change. On the contrary, if anyone should be able to muster the faith in the God of Tomorrow to trust the move from one generation to the next, it is surely religious life.

It will be another generation who opens the promised land, yes, but only because we had faith enough in this one to learn from the past and then accept the rest of the journey.

"What we will be has not yet been revealed" (1 John 3:2).

Chapter 3

WHAT'S THE POINT OF SUCH A LIFE IN A WORLD LIKE OURS?

"Many persons have a wrong idea of what
constitutes true happiness. It is not attained
through self-gratification but through
fidelity to a worthy purpose."

Helen Keller

The discussion is always an intense one. Why religious life at all? As one woman put it, "Why commit myself to a religious community with so much uncertainty if, as a layperson, I can (1) develop my spiritual life anywhere; (2) develop a spiritual community anywhere; (3) practice deep meaningful spirituality in any community of lay or religious people; (4) practice financial and social independence; and (5) have the ability to engage in romantic relationships? Isn't it enough to be a serious layperson and live a good life? Isn't that really the same thing?"

The questions are serious ones. Good ones. Important ones. They are exactly the questions every religious must face and answer. And my own personal answer to them is, "Right. You can certainly do all of that in the married or the single state. And by all means, if that's what you want, do it."

There is no other foolproof answer.

Those questions are not equations to be worked out. They cannot be determined by any number of scientific studies. They are not a matter of genetics. These "religious" types range from people as unalike as St. Frances of Rome and Teresa of Avila, as St. Dominic and Thomas Merton. There is, in other words, no such thing as a religious personality "type."

Just as there is no way to really know, at least at first, if you are the type who could be being called to enter a religious order.

Instead, the answer is disarming for its simplicity. The fact is that only you know if this kind of life, a commitment that calls for and is grounded in total concentration on the spiritual dimension of life, is the kind of life that tugs at you for response. If giving yourself to a life that is deeply contemplative and at the same time unstintingly active feels like the fullness of life to you, then you must give these questions serious attention. If what a thing means inside of you is more important to you than what it looks like to others, then you must resolve this now or spend the rest of your life wrestling with it. If the lifestyle you are looking for is a call to change the world, there are fifteen hundred years of history to prove that this lifestyle does just that.

The call to courage and single-minded service is not a call to leave the world. It is a call to change the world. Step right up.

The truth is that twelve years after I entered religious life I found myself confronted with a question, the answer to which I had long taken for granted years before. I was almost thirty. Was this the place I really wanted to be? Should I be thinking of starting a family? The struggle between the two plagued me for months. I could imagine a family; I simply could not imagine myself out of a monastery. The fact is, I came to understand, that I am simply "this kind of person." The magnet in me pointed to the prayer life, the life of prophetic witness, the life of the spiritual love affair with God and the world that God created. With the apostle Peter, the only answer that rang over and over again in my head when I asked myself if I should leave was, "Lord, to whom shall I go?" And no answer came back because the answer was already there.

It's all about deciding for yourself what "kind of a person" you are. What kind of life you're seeking. What kind of legacy you want to leave with the talents you've been given.

It isn't that deciding to enter was easy when I found myself face-to-face with it. But it was always the underlying riptide of my life. What else could possibly supply for it?

Yes, I had been born in a generation deluded by the canons of the Church into thinking that there was such a thing as "higher" and "lower" vocations. But I never really believed it. And my mother was about as high a spiritual level as anybody could get. And the Sisters, of course, who were my sacred idols for their strength and their clear-mindedness, were the models to me of the totally dedicated life. But I also knew that everyone was called by God to do something special, something only we could each do well, whatever it was. The Scriptures were clear: We were all meant to "minister" to someone, somewhere, somehow. But, in the end, it's all a matter of where we fit, what we love, and what we're made for that will determine how well we do it.

And this fit me. It is decades later and I still find the life both developmental and deeply satisfying. Not the work it does but the kind of life it is has nourished my soul and stretched my vision. It is my entire life and the only bridge that could possibly take me to the mystical dimension of life.

Religious life is about a great deal more than the forms it has taken—as important as these may be. Religious life starts in the heart and soul and mind of the seeker. It becomes the light within them that witnesses to the God who is with us in the midst of darkness, in the jumble of the mundane. It is both the driving force of the search for the Spirit and the vision of the possible that leads religious to make those things visible in the present. It is more than

15

a canonical life; it is a charismatic life. Or, as the disciples of an earlier time asked the old monastic, "Holy One, what's the difference between knowledge and enlightenment?" And the Holy One replied, "When you have knowledge, you light a torch to find the way. When you have enlightenment, you become a torch to show the way."

Enlightenment begins with the development of the presence of God within us and leads us to become the torch that is a trustworthy guide to many. That is the essence of religious life, whatever its form. As the ancients taught, it is as a "cloud of witnesses" that religious travel the world, being in themselves a sign of the possibility of God-ness in us and around us. Here and now.

The truth is that people join religious communities in order to be able to do together what they cannot possibly do alone. Both the personal discipline required of the religious life and the great public efforts required for the humanizing of humanity beg for support. Religious life gives a person a tried spiritual tradition to trust in. It gives models along the way. It gives the support we need on the days we falter on the path or in the work or at the center of the heart. As we all do everywhere at some time or another.

More than that, in community we each become part of the great anonymous corporate voice that cries out as one for the poor, for the oppressed, for the invisible, for the lost, for the ones with no one to care for them. In fact, who alone would have the strength for it?

In a world of public inequity, of personal invisibility, of national inequality, it takes great courage to mount the public watchtower and sound the trumpet when the will of God for the human condition needs attention. That task cannot be done alone. In community life, the single voice is amplified, is raised to the power of hundreds.

One thing we know: Religious life existed from the earliest moments of the early Christian community. We are over twenty centuries away from that now. So we must ask ourselves whether or not, in the plethora of this history, there is any real essence to be found at all. Or is what we have simply a cacophony of goodwill?

The earliest known groups of women dedicated to the pursuit of the God-life in the Christian tradition were called the "The Order of Widows." In an era when women had no agency, they took agency of their own souls. If nothing else, they were an early sign of the call of women to a special role in the Christian dispensation.

Since then, for each of almost twenty-one centuries, men and women religious have been the pulse and heartbeat of the Church. Religious life stood in the center of every community, another sign, a different kind of sign, to keep alive the model of Jesus, a voice for the oppressed and a sign of the living presence of the God of Love.

They were the living memory of Jesus walking through time. Our time. Carrying our burdens with us. Calling the world to see what is missing for many if God's will for us all is to be as real for others as it is for us.

Indeed, this single-minded dedication to a life devoted to public expression of the spiritual life has taken many forms. But its forms are not its essence. Its essence is its common devotion to the heart and soul and vision of God for humankind.

It is as if in every era the spiritual guardians of that century handed on a torch to the next, saying as each group waxed and waned, "Carry on...Be the light...Show the way...Companion the lonely...Succor the sick...Console the suffering...Uphold the lowly..." until this life melts into the next and compassion has flowered into eternal consolation.

But maybe even more important than a history of religious life and community care by Christians in the West is the fact that all the great spiritual traditions—Hindu, Buddhist, Jewish and Muslim—have also done the same. The religious figures of each culture have been its spiritual bellwethers. Gandhi was a Hindu; the Dalai Lama a Buddhist; Abraham Joshua Heschel, a Jewish rabbi; Hafiz, a Sufi; Thomas Merton, Mother Teresa, and Dietrich Bonhoeffer, Christians. In each case, religious figures have both

17

preserved the mystical dimension of the spiritual life as well as inserted it into the issues of the age.

Clearly, life dedicated to spiritual development and the coming of the reign of God is universal. It is the other side of the story of Creation. It is the part that calls us all to create a world of love in the here and now. It is about modeling what it means to go on cocreating what God gave us to finish.

And we all must do it, in every possible way: As married partners devoted to the success of the human enterprise. As single seekers whose family is the world. As women and men religious who live together dinned by the word of God to be a loud and clear voice of the prophets for peace and justice.

Religious life is the story of those who go through the world holding the Scriptures in one hand and their community Office book in the other. Why? Because this, they have decided, is their whole life. There is nothing else to which they have been called. And that is precisely why I, with them, decided that religious life was the only life that was really right for me.

"Lord, to whom can we go? You have the words of eternal life" (John 6:68).

Chapter 4

WHY JOIN A GROUP WHEN YOU CAN BE ON YOUR OWN?

"We have all known the long loneliness and we
have learned that the only solution is love and
that love comes with community."

Dorothy Day

More people live alone in the United States now than ever before
in history. It touches every generation of us. Young people get their
first apartment as an inarguable show of maturity; older people
downsize or find themselves some kind of single again; professionals
move into walk-ups in big cities far from home so they can live
closer to work, get there earlier, stay later, get promoted faster.

The apartment and, of course, the car, are the natural by-
products of a culture devoted to independence, intent on progress.

The one problem is that "independence" doesn't really exist
and the definition of progress is anybody's guess in a world where
companies close as fast as they open and the climb to the top is far
too often a climb to nowhere. As a result, as part of the modern

corporate scramble, families are splashed all over the country, all over the world. The definition of family as mother, father, and two children is no longer considered *de rigueur.* Toddlers are being introduced to far-flung cuttings of the family tree on FaceTime. There are no cousins, aunts, or uncles around. The boundaries of family life have gotten smaller over the years.

This is where communities of religious come in, as well. I learned that very young and very quickly.

I remember my first night in the monastery. Communal sleeping quarters, a feature of nineteenth-century family life, had disappeared decades ago in the United States but was still taken for granted in convents.

In this setting, "privacy" was more a property of silence than of space and though dormitories were seen as an aspect of "community," they were a relatively bogus one. Sleeping in a dormitory together does not a community make.

We discovered, with the rest of the world, that privacy encouraged the development of a more real sense of self than the mere presence of other people could. The personal opportunity for contemplation and reflection freshened the soul. The psychological importance of having the space and time to let stress slip away at the end of one day so that the next day's work would be welcome was more of a gift to the upbuilding of community than togetherness for its own sake ever was.

And so, along the way, in the course of transition from one era of religious life to another, after the Renewal Council that generated such updating, we discovered whole new insights into the real meaning of community. We learned that it was about a great deal more than conformity and herding and anonymity. Indeed, we had been schooled in the regimen of conventionality and knew its deficiencies: this way to walk, this way to sit, this way to hold an Office book in chapel. Those things we came to realize did not touch the heart or bring the kind of connections it takes to bind the soul of a community together.

Community, we learned the hard way, was about understanding the power and the gift of differences. It was about coming to understand the real meaning of Creation. We were not all made alike; we were simply all made human—in all the variances that implied. We were, in this monastery, a picture of the world and all its strangers up close and personal.

In fact, an aunt of mine was incensed to learn that I was going to a Benedictine high school on the east side of town. "You don't want to go there," she said with an edge of disdain in her voice, which meant that since the academy was on the edge of a Polish neighborhood, the student body would most likely be more Polish than most. Those were not my people, in other words. Why would I even think of going there? Oh, how we could put on airs...

But, in the end, I entered the novitiate there, as well, and woke up that first morning long ago in the middle of the League of Nations. This community was made up of everyone from everywhere: It was of German origin, but now the ethnic backgrounds of the members were multiple: Polish, indeed, but Irish, Italian, German, Slovak, Russian and "other," as well.

Community life, I began to understand, was the Sacrament of Strangers. We had come together from all these little towns and from far-flung states and ethnic backgrounds to prove that the world could, if we wanted it badly enough, become whole. But becoming whole would require a good bit of being willing to be born again in unsettling new ways.

Out of many cultures we needed to develop a communion of hearts. We were all to be about the gospel together. We would need to prove that, like all the foreigners that Jesus took in, we could live with and grow with one another, too: the Romans, Samaritans, Gentiles, lepers, and tax collectors of our own time.

We would need to realize that the small local priorities and ethnicities we had learned before this would need to be melded into one Great Heart for the entire world. We could leave no one out. We were meant to take everyone in. We were meant to find in the gospel common purpose together. We were meant to be a community.

And that would mean learning to respect differences, to recognize and encourage gifts other than our own, to select and honor leaders from outside our ethnicities, to respect the needs and feelings of others for which we had no natural sensitivity. I learned quickly that if we really intended to teach the world what community was, we would first have to learn it ourselves.

"What is a religious community?" I asked myself over and over again through the years: As we struggled with the polarization, both internal and public, that strained the community almost to the breaking point as we trekked out of the nineteenth century into the twentieth. As we began to develop new ways of being a community in public. As we ourselves fumbled with the notion of community as we stopped making teachers out of everyone and began to actually encourage Sisters to follow their own gifts in order to be their most impactful selves.

Community, we learned, is a way of facing the world together—as one, yes, but made up of a hundred pieces.

It is immersion in a sea of personal differences, of "sisters" alike only in their commitment to the gospel, who had pledged to help one another do it, too.

Of all the qualities and characteristics of religious life, this one—community—so often goes unattended to and unnoticed. Yet without it there is nothing of real community about it at all. After all, how can we talk community to a world unless we model it ourselves? How can we be it unless we do it? How can it be real for anyone else if it is not real for us? And if not, how can we possibly make it open to those others, whoever they are, wherever they come from, but who are looking to us to provide the home away from home that is everybody's home once they get there?

If a universal home is what you're looking for, community is it. It points us to the heavenly home where no one is excluded and everyone is welcome—if we make them so.

"The disciples came to him and said, 'This is a deserted place, and the hour is now late; send the crowds away so that they may go into the villages and buy food for themselves.' Jesus said to them, 'They need not go away; you give them something to eat'" (Matt 14:15–16).

Chapter 5

HOW CAN A LOVELESS LIFE POSSIBLY BE A HEALTHY ONE?

"Though friendship is not quick to burn,
it is explosive stuff."

May Sarton

The trouble in today's world is that people act as if there were only one kind of love in the world. And so, some are inclined to overlook the other two. In our case, that leaves out the most impacting of them all.

The sound of a baby crying had become common in our monastery. Sister Judith, a woman with a soft voice and an even softer look on her face, had a reputation by now. She was known across the social service network in the city as "the Sister who took in babies" from the time of birth until the completion of a successful adoption.

This particular morning, Judith was at her desk in the finance office organizing invoices, as usual. Next to her desk the electric swing seat rocked methodically back and forth. Visitors to the monastery were delighted to see it but also regularly startled by it. This baby was the child of a drug addicted mother and the baby showed the signs of it. She fussed and screamed, sobbed and kicked a bit. What was a baby, any baby, let alone one like this, doing in a monastery?

Sister Judith stopped at every point, took the baby out of the swing, hugged her to her shoulder and walked up and down the hall till the sobs lost their energy and the agitation slowed to a halt.

Was she spoiling the baby? Not according to the latest research.

The amygdala of a baby's brain, science tells us, only completes its development after birth. But this happens best, the documents recount, only if the baby has the attention and affection necessary to stimulate it. And then, the most striking element of all: the development of the amygdala determines the difference between a child that grows up peaceful and one that demonstrates serious agitation or aggression throughout life.

That baby had a special need for someone to hold her as the withdrawal from her birth mother's drug addiction went slowly, painfully on. This baby had a particular need for this attention. This was clearly a very important ministry.

And at one level, it was very true—Sister Judith did "take in babies." At the same time, every baby she took in meant that the rest of us took in another baby, too. The community enabled it, supported it, and saw it as a direct outgrowth of our own corporate commitment to world peace. And why not?

After all, religious life is all about love, isn't it? As least as I have known it, it is.

It was the Sisters who took a very special place in my own life growing up. In those days, just being an only child was enough to bring strange stares and a feeling of defect. But this family, euphemistically called a "mixed marriage," was also riven by difference of religion and an excess of alcohol, a veritable witches' brew of prejudices fueled by drink and accented by violence. But with the Sisters I was both safe and cared for. In fact, without those years, I doubt that I could ever have walked so confidently between the polarities that religion presented then. Later, it was the Sisters who identified my penchant for language and nurtured it unceasingly. Without them I doubt that I would ever have become a writer, for instance. But they saw the gifts and, just like Sister Judith and this child, gave them very special attention.

Most interesting of all, perhaps, is that these were celibates who were giving their lives to the care of children. Isn't that a contradiction? If there is a contradiction, it lies in that fact that in those days a Sister's ministry was imposed, not chosen. But as change came, new insights came about that, as well. We came to understand that no work was foreign to us that came from concern and no work was proper for us that came more from the demands of institutionalism than the outbursts of love.

This first kind of love, love that culminates in service, is the love of Jesus for the forgotten, the care of Jesus for the uncared for, the concerns of Jesus for the deprived.

The second kind of love, the physical bonding of two people, is life giving. It is meant to give life both to the world and to the relationship.

True, religious life is not about sex, but it is all about love. The confusion comes from the fact that contemporary society is all about sex and thinks it's the same as love. The truth is that love is much deeper than physical excitement. Otherwise, how do we account for the fact that sex is, at best, only a small part of even the healthiest life. Only love that is beyond sex—more than sex—is about forever.

If sex were essential to love, then sickness, age, accident, and disability would be the end of it. But the truth is that sex can't keep a marriage together and neither can it end it. Not a real marriage.

If anything, religious life, too, is a sign of real love. It is proof that love is possible without sex and that love that asks for nothing in return is the purest, most dramatic love of all.

It is love itself, not sex, that is the bond of life. Which explains why it is as real in a religious community as it is in any marriage.

Sex will challenge the celibate, yes, because that is the nature of nature and the measure of growth. Sex will put celibacy under trial. Sex will question its breadth and depth of love forever. But sex will never be as consuming as love for its own sake.

This kind of love, the third kind of love, is friendship at its highest, deepest level.

Strong communities are made of those chains of friendship that cross generations and tie us to one another, however distant we may seem. Like the ropes of mountain climbers, the love of Sisters holds us fast when everything in life around us—our health, our work, our very faith, our spiritual life, and the depression that comes with change and loneliness—threatens to leave us unmoored in life.

It is holy friendship that grows us up emotionally. When, still unsure of ourselves, we become too needy of another's attention, it is the warmth of the community that makes the journey to new growth possible. Then, it is holy friendship that shows us the way down from such imprisoning heights, that helps us through our insecurities, that shows us the love and stability that community brings.

When we reach for the stars and fail, it is the presence of a loving other, the Sister friend, who helps us stay the road. In that comfort we find enough inner strength to get up and go on despite the disappointment or the loss. In this kind of protective love and holy wisdom, we learn that there is more love around us than we ever knew we had.

When we are bruised by policies or changes or disappointments or disillusionments in community life, it is one holy friendship that is enough to help us see the larger picture, the way back into the group.

When we feel deep differences between us and the community, it is often love for the others that keeps us there in the midst of our differences, because down deep, we know we belong. It enables us to see that love for the community is more important than our being able to agree with the community's present position on a current topic. The issues at hand and all the various positions on them will come and go in community life, but the people who make the community a community are our bedrock.

All those situations are real and all that love is true because life is simply like that, wherever we are, whatever we become, stage after stage of our lives. The challenge of love is to go through each phase of our lives and come out even more committed, more holy, and more spiritually mature than we were when we began. And that is the task of religious life, marital life, and independent life alike.

During the years of change and renewal when life careened from point to point, from change to change, and community feelings, parish feelings, and family feelings ran deep and divided, we found ourselves where so many other groups had also come. Whole numbers of community members everywhere were considering leaving religious life and either starting another one or simply giving up religious life entirely. The issue for us this time was whether or not we would all wear a veil. The vote was dangerously close. Then someone suggested that we change the vote from the matter at hand and make a different kind of decision. Instead of trying to resolve the issue once and for all, we were asked another question, a simple question. We were to decide if we would trust our Sisters to do what they each thought best for their own growth at this particular time.

I remember looking slowly around the room at the community in solemn chapter assembled. Their faces were drawn, their bodies were taut, and now, at that suggestion to personalize the question, the shock was apparent, too. People moved uncomfortably in their seats. This was not the Rubicon they were expecting. The vote was 121 to 1 in favor of trust and love. Community had triumphed over conformity one more important time.

It had been a "lover's quarrel" and love—holy friendship—had healed it, had reconciled it at the root, had demonstrated what is and is not important in a community.

WHAT ARE YOU LOOKING FOR?

Let there be no doubt about it: Love is of the essence of religious community life. Sex is neither its synonym, nor its cure. Its cure lies in learning that love in a religious community is wider and deeper than love that is particularized, is located in only one person, and is meant to be a world unto itself, good as that may be.

Then someday, like your married friends, you come to know the power of death. And then, without doubt, in the midst of the pain of loss, you also know you have loved.

No, this kind of love does not create its own family, but it does allow a group to take everyone in, even a baby maybe, and so be the love of God that is needed here and now.

"Love one another as I have loved you" (John 15:12).

Chapter 6

WHEN DID COMPLIANCE BECOME A VIRTUE?

"Conventionality is not morality."

Charlotte Brontë

Two images flashed through my mind when I read the writer's question. The woman was middle age and had been thinking of entering a religious order for years. But there were a few expectations of religious life she simply could not yet reconcile with her own situation. The most serious of them was obedience. Or as she put it, "At least not at my age."

The quip reminded me of the first image I'd seen of the fall of the old notions of obedience. In this cartoon, a screaming, squealing, foot-stomping child about six years old was being dragged by a mother to the desk of the local nun. "Do something," she was shouting, "He won't do a thing I tell him." It was the image of a generation in revolt. Even at the age of six, the child wanted to be part of the decision-making process in life.

Obedience, the cartoon was clear, is not about trivia. It is about the emergence of moral agency in us all.

Frankly, I couldn't think of a better way to explain the issue than that. If obedience is about turning adults into children, what good is religious life at all? This enterprise called "the vowed life" is definitely not an infantile undertaking, not a puerile, thoughtless thing. This life is not about kid stuff.

The second image came out of a tome called *The Sayings of the Desert Monastics*, a collection of the spiritual wisdom of third-century monks. A favorite exercise in the formation of young monks, we're told, was directing them to water a stick until further notice. Sometimes for years. Or at least until they stopped questioning the practice.

It was an image that stuck. There was another way to understand this story, I came to realize as the years of reflection went by, but that was not the interpretation we got then. The willingness to stay at something, even though nothing seems to be gained by doing it, is the virtue of those who have given their lives to long-lasting or lost causes, yes. And they may indeed by valorous—as in "The poor we have always with us." But to do something inane just because authority requires it without rhyme or reason is entirely another.

The portrait of silent, unquestioning nuns lingers still in our own time. In the first place, affirmation of that kind of morality is not only wrong, but the very thought of it is an aberration of the vowed life. And worse, it is very bad theology.

Years ago, when I was a young novice, they didn't spend much time on the vow of obedience. "When you're told to do something, you do it," they told us. It was that simple. After all, what else was there to say about it? This is where that first image of a monk watering a stick came in. It was supposed to impress on us that we were to question nothing, however foolish it might seem. God, they assured us, would reward our faithful—and, it seemed to me, inane if not wanton—compliance.

The spiritual books of the era called that kind of thing "blind obedience" and applauded the virtue of it. But I wondered.

In fact, I had the temerity to ask the first question: If I'm told to do something that I know is wrong, what do I do then? And the answer I got was right out of the books. "All you have to do is to do what you're told," the novice director said, closing the discussion before it could get started. "You keep the Rule and the Rule will keep you," which meant, of course, that it wasn't the act itself, whatever it might be, that measured my morality. What would make me holy, apparently, was learning never to question at all. It was about turning my soul over to someone else. I thought about that for a while and my answer was "No, thank you."

When I look back, it wasn't so much the things I did in the name of obedience that I regret. What I regret is what I *never* did as a result of a theology like that. I never protested a war, for instance, since I had learned to obey the state, as well, whatever the nature of its killings. I never did anything to contest racism, despite the fact that our downtown monastery was right in the center of a black neighborhood. I never called out the sexism of the Church, at least not then.

But it wasn't long before the gospel overtook the old canons on religious life.

As one pyramid after another of white male privilege and patriarchy came under scrutiny, I saw the flaws in the theology, too. The obedience of Jesus who contested with the Scribes and Pharisees, the Jesus who broke the Sabbath to heal the sick, the Jesus who overturned the givens of his society was not a model of the vow of control and "blind obedience." Obedience was clearly a call to personal responsibility. To conscience. To choice. To the kind of accountability that no clerical clothing, no title, no vow of irresponsibility could ever redeem.

Of course, obedience was about keeping the law, but it was not about keeping just "any" law decreed by those who claimed to be in charge of everybody else. The law religious are called to keep is the Law of God, the law of the gospel, the law of the Christ who was crucified for refusing to obey the godless legislation of the time.

The call of religious life is to understand the model of life to which, as religious, we have pledged ourselves. The very meaning of the word *obedire*—out of which comes the English word *obedience*—is to listen. We vow to listen to one another, to listen to the call of the great questions of the world, to listen to life, to listen to the experts, to listen to the call of our spiritual traditions, to listen to the saints among us, to listen to the wisdom figures over us, and always to listen to the call of God to the heart of the world so that "we may all have life and have it more abundantly."

In my monastery, we work through major positions together knowing that each of us must do what we must do, both together and alone, to make the gospel real. As a community together, we take a corporate commitment "to be a healing presence and prophetic witness for peace by working for sustainability and justice, especially for women and children." These are all great issues of the time and people come to them out of multiple experiences and backgrounds. In fact, we each grow into them an insight at a time.

Has it been difficult to arrive at those positions together? Sometimes, yes. So we have had to work at them even harder knowing that responsible choice is a part of the vow of obedience. We know very well that, in the end, conscience is personal and sacrosanct. So some of our Sisters marched in Selma, were arrested in protest of the Vietnam War, are currently totally involved in protesting the amassing of nuclear weapons, recognizing the Christian commitment to ecological responsibility, and aiding in the awareness of sexual issues, feminism, women's rights, equality, and the plight and policies that affect immigrants.

They speak, write, march, petition, protest, and hold prayer vigils with the support of their communities. Why? Because racial equality, social justice, and the integrity of the modern Church itself rests on the world's position on globalism, LGBTQ people, women's issues, and the elimination of war. Because these all demand the kind of obedience Jesus modeled. These are all, at base, spiritual issues and so religious cannot, with authenticity, ignore them. And they are not—to this very day.

Meanwhile, we just keep growing together, growing more, growing more deeply, thanks to the insights we each bring to every question. Nobody waves a wand or snaps a finger to get us all in line at the same time. But what we know is that if we take the vow of obedience seriously, it may cost us something, yes, but it will deepen us, grow us, too. By listening to one another, asking the hard questions, taking things one person, one step at a time, and supporting one another as we each develop spiritually and at our own pace, we will listen our way into the will of God. We will have become "obedient" to the gospel message.

We will have learned that the moral witness of obedience is not simply about keeping institutional customs or organizational dictates, however important and necessary these may be to a community's lived experience. Rather, we will have learned that obedience is what is meant to bring us to full moral stature as adults. Then, as a result, we will be a very obedient community—no matter how many different ways we each decide to respond to these challenges together.

"And he said, 'Let anyone with ears to hear listen!'" (Mark 4:9).

Chapter 7

WHAT'S THE USE OF SUCH AN UNCOMMON COMMON LIFE?

"The greatness of a community is most accurately measured by the compassionate actions of its members."

Coretta Scott King

I need to be clear in this conversation of ours. I'm trying to help you understand the foundation on which religious life exists, the breadth of spiritual vision it takes to dedicate your life to trying to live so simply, so openheartedly.

I'm trying to sketch out for you what life looks like from the inside of a religious order. I'm trying to answer your basic questions about religious life in this day and age. Some other time you may want to trace the history of it, but for now your knowing what it is about religious life that has the power to transform is what's important, I think.

So, we've talked about what being a religious implies for your attitude toward human community, as in who's welcome and who isn't, for instance. Without that how can we possibly, any of us, walk in the way of Jesus the Obedient One in this world?

We've dealt, too, with the place of love in a celibate community and the meaning of that for the world. I've tried to make the point that love is essential to the health and quality of a religious order and that, contrary to the modern era's obsession with sex, love without sex is the most common kind of love in the world. Like Jesus, religious simply pledge themselves to be the public lovers of the age, as well, rather than its ever-faithful partners.

We've looked at the kind of obedience to which we bind ourselves for the sake of the world. I've tried to make the point that it is conscience, not commitment to organizational guidelines (necessary as these may be), to which we vow ourselves.

It is, in other words, a gospel-centered way of life. But it's more than theory, more than theological assertions. It's about living differently than the world around us. It assumes a different worldview, an entirely different set of values than the ones the culture holds, a different way of seeing what it means to live a good and happy life.

It is, then, a gospel-centered lifestyle as well as a gospel-centered theology. Like road signs in strange territory, our lives point life in another direction. A countercultural direction. It is a little plied perspective of which the world around us considers foolish, but Jesus made it the sign of hope in a hopeless world.

All of this is wrapped up in what we call the common life. Life in common is life lived for others as well as for the self and it is demonstrated through the community of goods. But it is the community of goods that is distinctly and stingingly anti-American.

In this age, we have thousands upon thousands of healthy, hearty, professionally effective and well-trained individuals, men and women religious, who never earn a penny in their own name. Instead, they pool their money, and whatever exists after the community's bills are paid, they, as a community, invest in the welfare of others. But in a money economy, that part of the gospel message "seems like foolishness to a world" that is mired in personal profit, individualism, and independence. To understand how essentially countercultural that kind of life is, think about it this way: This is a life that exists to sustain others. It is based on sufficiency rather than profit. It concerns itself instead with justice for others, either by enabling them to achieve it or by themselves advocating for the needs of others. It is a life lived in the name of justice for all.

Yet, in the midst of economic insecurity and inequity, governments, including our own, are more and more ignoring the problem—or making it. They may legislate for a minimum wage, but they seldom provide a decent wage or a living wage for those whose paychecks and benefits cannot provide those things. As a result, jobs, subsidized housing, food stamps, medical care, and the education needed to enable the poor to improve their own life circumstances simply dry up and shrivel away.

With the concentration of resources at the top, what is left for those who really need it? The poor stay poor and, ironically, are every day more and more reviled for it.

In my own town, the poorest in Pennsylvania, inner-city children live almost entirely on cheap fast food. "I never knew you were supposed to eat three meals a day," a little girl told our Sisters and the newspaperman who was there to report on our opening of a soup kitchen for children.

We are clearly a culture where rugged individualism has taken over the gospel and its warning that when we fail to take care of "the least of these" we fail to do the will of God. Instead we "hoard grain in barns," we amass money we will never use and do not need for ourselves alone.

Two kinds of people put their lives to the task of doing the gospel. The first are wealthy philanthropists and the conscientious and generous middle class, who, out of their own resources, provide the programs and services, the opportunities and investments in the future that a humane, human environment demand.

WHAT ARE YOU LOOKING FOR?

In the Middle Ages, before governments began to recognize their role in human development, we called such people "patrons." Without them then and without them now there would be far less formal education and even less music, art, and public services. Our own inner-city art house is subsidized by donations, too. The people in the city know the value of planting culture in the hearts of the children on the streets. But as long as the government itself continues to withdraw from that kind of support, we are living on charity rather than justice.

The problem is that there are simply too few individuals capable of bearing the total cost for what governments should be doing for all its citizens. If we want strong nations instead of a wealthy upper class oblivious to the economic slavery of the poor, we must discover the need for national pooling of our money with more equity than we have now.

Otherwise, we must remember that of circumstances such as these, revolutions were made.

The second group of people who give of themselves to make life possible for others in the face of such massive deprivation are men and women religious. The response of religious life to a culture that ignores the poor is to create communities of care in which no one is rich but no one is poor either. Religious congregations everywhere have planted themselves in one ethnic community after another in order to feed children's minds and souls as well as their bodies. My own has been in the center of the city for over 150 years. Clearly, Jesus was right: "The poor we have always with us."

In our case, our own community has seen one minority after another come and go—German immigrants, Polish-speaking émigrés looking for land and labor, African American families struggling to get by, Vietnamese refugees, displaced Muslims, and Bhutanese exiles. They have all been lifted up and out of our neighborhood, due at least in part to our presence there. They leave it; we don't. When they leave it, we applaud the fact that they can. When the next group moves in, we applaud that, too.

What's the Use of Such an Uncommon Common Life?

Religious orders are a network of congregations and communities that pool their assets and share their goods with everyone they touch, both within their walls and outside of them.

The difference between wealthy philanthropists and vowed religious is that philanthropists give charity to the poor; religious live and work among the dispossessed they serve in the hope that presence itself can be a sign of care, encouragement, and equality.

But to do that, religious life confronts the most sensitive nerve of them all. We must have the courage to relinquish private ownership.

I remember as a child my mother and father parceling out my dad's paycheck every payday. They were making sure that I would never doubt that my needs were important to them, too. Religious communities do the same. Yet, of all the things we do, this may be the one that goes most against the spiritual grain of a public geared to getting more and more and more of the public slice of "success," of property, of personal profit.

Common ownership tests our faith, our trust, and our freedom. As Abbot Zosimas said in the fifth century, "The soul has as many masters as it has passions." In a world of wealth with governments who protect its privatization, it is not so much the things we possess that are our problem as it is which of them possesses us. What is it precisely that is nailing our feet to the floor, that makes it impossible for us to find spiritual freedom enough to take care of those who have little but whose work makes wealth for the rest of us?

Indeed, common ownership is a many-sided shaper of the soul.

Common ownership teaches the religious a sense of "enoughness." It shows what we can have together that not only provides for our necessities but also for the common joys of life: the cars we can use together for a trip, the concerts we can attend that feed our souls, the films that keep us in touch with the rest of the world, days on the beach, hamburgers together, ongoing educational opportunities, time with the family, whatever. And they all come out of all the efforts of everyone in the community.

WHAT ARE YOU LOOKING FOR?

The common life teaches us that public poverty is a public tragedy, but that voluntary poverty liberates. It frees us from the drug of accumulation that weighs us down and slows our steps and makes it impossible for us to travel lightly through life, to be where we need to be when we need to be there.

Most of all, the common life is an excursion into public responsibility for one another. It sees that the elderly and infirm have the care and the life experiences that they, too, need to live the endgame well. To hold all things in common leaves no one out. On the contrary, because we all provide for one another, it makes Sisterhood real and the common good a living thing.

In this world we can see it happening: Fewer and fewer have more and more. More and more have less and less. But, in community, hoarding is not a virtue, and stewardship, the care of goods, is a way of life.

To choose the common life, it takes the courage to believe that freedom from possessiveness and God's loving care can go hand in hand. More than that, it is those with whom we have pledged our lives who are its signs, both to us and to the world around us, that there is such a thing as the common good.

It is that kind of hope that Jesus gave the poor of his own time, and it is to the poor of our time that we must give the same. We must be a sign that as part of the human community, they, too, must be part of our lives, part of our own spiritual growth as well as our spiritual commitment.

"[Jesus] said to him [the crippled man], 'Do you want to be made well?' The sick man answered him, 'Sir, I have no one to put me into the pool…'" (John 5:6–7).

42

Chapter 8

WHAT'S ALL THE PRAYING ABOUT?

> "Prayer does not change God, but it
> changes him [or her] who prays."
>
> *Søren Kierkegaard*

I've heard it said that some things go without saying. Well, if that's true, then this concern for the place of prayer in the individual life must surely be one of them. However we may assume the idea of personal spirituality, the import of it is immeasurable. Prayer is the fountain out of which flows concern for others, a sense of the presence of God in everything, and the stretch of the soul to do and be more and more. To ignore the place of prayer in life, or to take it for granted, is to undermine its very existence.

The truth is that prayer is not "a part" of religious life. Prayer is its very foundation, its inner breath. If the prayer life of the religious fails to grow with the years and the pressures out of which it arises are ignored, then both community life and ministry itself begin to wilt on the vine.

Prayer is, for the religious, a deep well in the center of a dry desert. In this world, life has run dry in its marathon search for achievement, security, and control. In a culture and a world such as this, where these values dwarf all others, it is a temptation that haunts religious life, as well.

It is so easy to begin to keep track of success, even in the spiritual life. We do a lot of counting, too: so many soup kitchens opened, so many volunteers signed up for the winter months, so many children enrolled in programs designed to keep them off the rough and drug-ridden streets, so many homeless sheltered every freezing night. But that is not what counts. Success is not our goal.

Jesus described the presence of God this way: "The blind receive their sight, the lame walk...and the poor have good news brought to them" (Matt 11:5). Clearly, what really counts in the lexicon of spirituality is simply being there in all those places with all those people who forever will need the food, the programs, the help. Being there is as much a spiritual need for us, as our presence may well be a spiritual need for them.

This life is a vocation, a lifestyle, in other words, a commitment to another way of being in the world. It is not simply another corporate enterprise. It is not a business.

The desire to secure our ministries, both spiritual and material, rather than forever begging other people to help us keep them alive, is an understandable one. But a dangerous one. Over the centuries, too many religious communities—to ensure their own existence—"stored grain in barns" rather than pouring out their own resources on an even needier poor. But security for its own sake is not a religious virtue. Our virtue is faith in the hundredfold. That we will be given what we need in order to go on helping others is basic, yes, but it is not a promise that we will become rich ourselves, as a result.

Finally, control is the great human pitfall. The attempt to make life right can lead to the attempt to define what is right for everyone else, too. The right way to do a thing, the right way for other people to act, knowing the right answers—meaning trying to sell our answers rather than learning to listen to the right questions—can taint the work of love with the odor of control. It is the call to remember that Jesus did not act either like Moses or the high priests. He simply brought the presence of God to the people. He never tried to control them as pay for having done so. He did not adopt the clerical culture of superiority and control that he saw around him.

And that's where prayer comes in. Prayer exposes us to ourselves. Prayer brings the religious into daily contact with the mind and model of Jesus and gives us something to strive for. Until, finally, over the years, one day at a time, this constant confrontation with goodness transforms us. Maybe that's why age and experience are such beguiling things in a religious community. To see people change as the years go by makes our own hope for conversion possible.

Daily prayer—serious daily prayer—brings us face-to-face with the heart of Jesus. It keeps us connected to the important things of life despite the trivia of dailiness. It engages us in a soul-wrestling match with ideas we have learned to ignore. Faced with the Jesus of the Gospels, we are plunged into the big questions of life: Who am I outside the public image? What do I really believe? Why do I really do what I do? It takes us beyond the recitals of rituals and centers us. It takes us out of the clamoring, competitive world in which we live to an awareness of what it is to be real inside, to be genuine, to be bound to the ground of life.

Prayer confirms us in our commitment. Like the disciples around Jesus, we see in him what life is meant to be about and we give ourselves to it again. In the light of the Gospels, how can we possibly forget the oppressed, ignore the needy, or do less than everything we can to make the world a loving place for the unloved?

Prayer shows us the way to our real selves, the self that seeks to be whole. It is the launching pad for our desire to be really holy rather than give in to our false selves that seek to be recognized and desire to be honored for the simple reason of being at all.

Prayer makes us real, makes us honest with ourselves, makes us simple and humble and true to what otherwise would be image and empty icon only.

WHAT ARE YOU LOOKING FOR?

Prayer leads us to where our gift of self is waiting always and needed most. It makes our work meaningful, holy, endless, untiring, a shaft of light in a dozen darknesses otherwise unattended without us.

Indeed, prayer immerses us in the cry of the Psalmist and the curse of the prophet. Then, we ourselves become both psalmist and prophet-in-waiting. We are suddenly, stolidly open to the pain they point out to us, and more, fearless about the cost it will exact of us if and when we respond to it.

Some years ago I asked a group of women new to religious life why they went to prayer. The answers were an exercise in catechetical propriety: To increase their love of God? No. To grow in the spiritual life? No. To become engaged with Scripture? No. No. No. One after another they went on reciting until they became irritated as well as frustrated. "Then why do we go to prayer?" one of them said, finally exasperated. "You go to prayer," I said slowly and carefully, "because the bell rang."

They got it. Prayer is a part of our lives. It is also a part of what it means to be in a community when we ourselves feel less intent on keeping the disciplines of the spiritual life alone. Then, all of religious life is geared to growing us up spiritually when we are least intent on growing ourselves.

In religious community, we carry one another to God. When the bell rings, we go with the crowd and become more and more immersed in God ourselves.

"I have prayed for you [, Simon,] that your own faith may not fail; and you, when once you have turned back, strengthen your brothers [and sisters]" (Luke 22:32).

Chapter 9

WHAT'S ALL OF THIS GOT TO DO WITH FOLLOWING JESUS?

> "The important thing is not to think much
> but to love much; and so do that
> which best stirs you to love."
>
> *Teresa of Avila*

The question of the day is a simple but potentially life-changing one: Why would anyone even bother to think about religious life today?

What is the value of doing something like that?

The truth is that we are all in the process of discovering again what it means to hold a charism in trust for the Church. First and foremost, the purpose of a charism—the gifts given to us by the Spirit in order to maintain the spirit of Jesus in the Church today—is not to hoard it and hide it for ourselves. The purpose of a religious charism is to share it, to give it away! We do not come to a religious order to hold these great religious charisms of charity or equality or justice or simplicity or community captive to some kind of ecclesiastical elitism by the less than the 1 percent of the Christian community who claim to own it.

WHAT ARE YOU LOOKING FOR?

Several ancient stories illuminate both the purpose and the spirituality of what it means to be a religious in this day and age.

The first of those stories is from the *Tales of the Desert Monastics*:

One day, Abbot Arsenius was asking an old Egyptian man for advice on something.

Someone who saw this said to him, "Abba Arsenius, why is a person like you, who has such great knowledge of Greek and Latin, asking a peasant like this for advice?" And Arsenius replied, "Indeed I have learned the knowledge of Latin and Greek, yet I have not learned even the alphabet of this peasant."

Abbot Arsenius knew what, as religious communities, as Church, and as people, we have forgotten for centuries: life is the world's greatest spiritual director. Our task is to learn from it so that we and our generation can do our part in steering this world to the wholeness of spirit it seeks.

In the end, each of us—lay as well as religious—carries within us a piece of the truth, but only a piece.

The Zen masters, too, tell a story about the nature of real religious commitment. The monk Tetsugen made his goal of life the printing of the Buddha's sutras in Japanese woodblocks. It was an enormous and expensive undertaking. But just as he collected the last of the necessary funds, the River Uji overflowed and left thousands homeless.

So Tetsugen, instead of using the money for the printing of the Scriptures in Japanese, spent all the money he'd collected on the homeless and began his fundraising again.

But the very year he managed to raise the money for a second time, an epidemic spread over the country. This time Tetsugen gave the money away to care for the suffering.

It took twenty more years to raise enough money to print the Scriptures in Japanese. Those printing blocks are still on display in Kyoto. But to this day, we're told, the Japanese tell their children that Tetsugen actually produced three editions of the sutras and that the first two editions—the care of the homeless, and the comfort of the suffering—are invisible but far superior to the third.

Clearly, the Zen masters know what we know: witness, not theory, is the measure of the spirituality we profess. What we do because of what we say we believe is the real mark of genuine spirituality. The link between deep spiritual development and an impacting spiritual life has been a constant.

Finally, St. Paul is very clear about our common obligation to be part of the Christian enterprise. "To each one," he teaches, "the manifestation of the spirit is given for the common good....It is given to each of us for the sake of the Christian community" (see 1 Cor 12:7–11).

These personal gifts of ours are not for our private little personal spiritual deserts alone. Together we are meant to be messengers, models, and makers of a whole new world of justice and love wherever we are.

The model of our own ancestors is more than clear about this:

Benedictines were visible in the healing work of hospices when sickness was considered a punishment for sin. They call to us today, then, to join hearts and hands and insights to be healing figures everywhere.

Religious were visible public witnesses to equality when the segregation of indigenous peoples and the enslavement of one people by another were thought to be God's will. They went then to lift the lives of those left behind. They continue to call us to join hearts and hands and insights now to make equality a sign of our own communities today.

Religious communities provided holy hospitality and security for pilgrims in religious guest houses as they traveled from one shrine to another in Europe. They call us yet to see Christ in everyone who comes through the doors of our homes and the arches of our monasteries.

Religious were visible in prophetic works as their communities recognized the plight of the working poor by providing food and care to families in earlier periods and by advocating legislation to deliver rather than restrict them now.

The charisms of the spirit are alive, in other words. They go on going on—as the memory of Jesus goes on going on in us.

These charisms are not ever complete. They are not frozen in time. They are not fixed and static, stagnant and stock-still. They leap with life. They never die. They are the electricity that powers every good in us. Ancient but immediate, they are dynamic, unfolding, and as necessarily new today as they were in the soul of those religious who went before us.

Charism, in other words, must be constantly rediscovered, and constantly reexpressed. Separately and alone and together, we must make it visible again in new ways. Together we must make it vocal again in the new language of a new time. My own community, for instance, closed the boarding school that opened in 1869 in order to develop a high school that could serve more students. Then, in 1988, in our time, we refined the project again, this time by turning it into an educational center and job training program for the poor and refugees. Now centered on the new poor, the heart of this old but new center beats the same today for its Buddhist and Muslim clients as it did for the German-Catholic immigrants for whom it first began. Yes, our students now are not children. In fact, they are adults. And yes, now they come in saris and burkas and hijabs rather than the blue and white uniforms of the age before this one, but their needs and their hopes are the same. And so are ours.

In the fifth century, when the Roman Empire broke down and Europe lay in ruin, Benedictinism was there to give both spiritual meaning and social organization to a people left without either a political center or spiritual guidance. That awareness is a cry to us to continue to bring basic human values to the center of every system.

When the emerging mercantile society began to consume the lives of the poor for the sake of a new economic system that robbed the poor of land but paid nothing for their labor, Franciscans lived in solidarity with the poor. That is a centuries-long cry to us to participate in the renewal and support of our own poverty-stricken societies.

When the new industrialization herded men into factory jobs but gave women nothing, women religious opened schools for girls to plant the seeds of a world without sexism that would someday be not only possible, but imperative. It is a call to us, too, to gather up today's forgotten ones, so that the vision of a more just and equal world may glow in our time, as well.

It is the depth of those spiritual traditions, the courage of those spiritual histories, the commitment of both women and men religious who brought us to this day. It is that spirit that we now hold in trust for those who seek to find. How, then, in the name of religious life, can we hide in our spiritual Jacuzzis, our pious spas, and say that we carry the charisms of those before us?

What is important to understand is not that all of us must have direct ministries with the poor. And not all of us can have the same ministry of any kind. I for one would not qualify as a religious if that were the case. I have never volunteered at a group home. I have never worked at a women's shelter. I have never served a cup of soup at our own soup kitchen. But I know who I am. My ministry is to help people understand that being Christian requires each of us to take responsibility to see that the cold are clothed, and the sick healed, and the hungry are fed. My ministry legitimizes the serving of soup.

The point is that each of us must do something to see that the poor can live a decent and dignified life, that God's will and Jesus's love are clear to everyone we meet.

Religious life is lived on a mountaintop of prayer, immersed in the cries of the Psalmist, challenged daily by the prophets, touched to the core by the demands of the gospel, and called by Jesus—liberator, redeemer, healer, and lover—to "Come follow me."

It is that call that leaves us with the question, Who are we struggling to liberate from the chains of rejection, poverty, and greed today?

WHAT ARE YOU LOOKING FOR?

The point is clear: we must each do what we can to provide what is needed of the presence of Jesus in our age.

Now is our time to carry these vibrant and world-changing charisms back into a world that needs them so badly.

"As you go, proclaim the good news, 'The kingdom of heaven has come near.' Cure the sick, raise the dead, cleanse the lepers, cast out demons. You received without payment; give without payment" (Matt 10:7–8).

Chapter 10

WHAT WOULD HAPPEN TO ME IF I JOINED A RELIGIOUS ORDER?

> "Life is a moving, breathing thing. We have to
> be willing to constantly evolve. Perfection
> is constant transformation."
>
> *Nia Peeples*

In the annals of monastic life, one ancient story stands out. "Holy One," the seeker said, "I have said all my little prayers, kept all the little fasts, honored all the commandments, now what must I do to be saved?" And the Holy One stood up, stretched out his arms, opened wide his fingers and said, "Why not be completely turned into fire?"

There are personal questions that must be factored into a decision to immerse yourself in a life centered on religious growth and lifestyle.

I am going to write some of them down, the ones that have been expressed the most in my presence. Years ago, people entered at a much younger age and were inclined to be more concerned about restrictions. Today's questions are broader, more concerned with human growth. But they are especially cogent in this day and age when people enter a religious order at a more developed stage of life, when they already know what it is to have been part of another lifestyle for years. These questions are, therefore, more pungent, more basic.

1. Should anyone enter an institution the future of which is so uncertain, so much in flux, as religious life seems to be now?

Life is not made up of certainties, much as we might wish otherwise. Life is made up of a series of events that test us, shape us, and ripen us.

The person who starts a business hopes it will succeed—but cannot guarantee it.

Marriages are celebrated with great expense and public splendor and then end as abruptly as they began. The divorce rate in America for first marriages astounds us.

Couples can plan for a number of children and then discover that it will be impossible for them to conceive at all. Suddenly they find that their image of family life comes down to the relationship between the two of them rather than their ideal of a family future.

Point: Life changes. It morphs from one form to another. And we with it. Every institution on the globe—government, medicine, education, business, and religion—is undergoing major shifts and turns as we all adjust to a world that is global, technological, and mobile. We are all evolving into something unforeseen.

As a result, none of us can be sure that tomorrow will look like yesterday. For those who seek the kind of stability that marked the second half of the twentieth century, it may for a while feel like a sad commentary on life that we are not able to secure (guarantee) its present forms, but it's not a tragic one. We learn about life—and even more about ourselves—from every experience. The world does not end in the process. We go on beyond change—most of us— wiser than before, more mature than we would possibly have been without the spiritual challenges with which life presents us.

All of those changes will affect all of us, and there will be nothing we can do to stop them. That is, after all, the spinning orbit in which we exist. Then, like the Israelites in the desert, we begin to see that God has been with us through it all. The awareness that life is a process, not an achievement, will be enough to expand our souls and open our hearts to the gifts life gives us in secret.

2. Do I have the kind of character and personality to be able to live a religious life?

If the religious life is where you fit, where you will grow most deeply and most fully, you will find its regularity and spiritual depth rich and fulfilling. It will take you down into yourself and bring you up again a freer, more centered person. If what you seek is to live life from the center of your soul rather than from a world full of things, this home is a simple but steadying one. If what you seek is the peace that comes from not always having to be in control, this home is a serene one. If what you seek is the desire to make life more loving for other people, as well as yourself, this home is a gentle and loving one. Then, you will know yourself to be at home here. Then you will grow here forever.

3. What will happen to me as a person in a group like this?

Buoyed up by the spiritual energy of the group, you will be transformed.

The tradition of the community sweeps us up and takes us beyond our public selves to that part of us that is forever in quest. We begin to see the whole arc of life. We see the past and its effect on us. Our community's burial plot is in the public cemetery, and as we put one Sister after another to rest there, we all take the occasion to walk the graves together.

There are more than 250 graves there now. They date back to 1856. But more than that, they are the graves of twenty-year-olds who died from tuberculosis in the cold northern winters. They are the graves of thirty-year-olds who came from Germany to support the German immigrants here and never saw their own homes and families again. They are the graves of Sisters who died in their late eighties and worked every day of their lives to support and sustain the rest of us. We knew them all. They had taught and raised so many of us. They were the Great Tradition.

They prayed and built and loved this community to life.

Even when we don't like having our work interrupted just to say a few psalms, even when we're too distracted to get much out of that day, we go to prayer remembering when they were in those pews with us. We go so that the drip, drip, drip of the psalms and the Gospels can finally, over time, wear down our natural resistance to ongoing growth as it did theirs. We go with the rest of the community that is also seeking the fullness of the God-life. Then, thanks to the community that carries us, we can open our hearts to the living and dynamic presence of God in the present moment.

What happens to us in religious life is that the spiritual routines, the traditions, the customs, and the fidelity of the community in which we make our vows evolve us. Slowly, surely we become the persons we came desirous of becoming. We become plunged into God and the world in such a way that where we are, life becomes more loving, more enriched for everyone.

4. Can anyone live a sexless life forever?

I understand the issue that underlies this concern, but it can't be answered because it's the wrong question. The question is, Can anyone live without love forever? And that answer is no. But no one is expected to live without love forever. On the contrary. We are made for love. We are each meant to be the voice of God's love for everyone we meet. No wonder we go through life looking for it ourselves.

The role of the celibate is to bring another kind of love into lives deprived of love or, worse, who are the victims of lovelessness. To love another is to be the presence of the God of Love for them. It is the greatest act possible to the human being.

At the same time, there are multiple shades of love: physical, spiritual, emotional.

Spiritual love emerges out of the deepest recess of our souls, but slowly. It takes a great deal of attention to develop and sustain it. Ironically, it is also often confused with the obvious. In its earlier stages it is inclined to depend on spiritual experiences, on incense and candles, rituals and recitations of prayers. But that is its planting time and needs a constant winnowing. The more mature we get, however—the less we are enamored of our own spiritual devices—the more real that love becomes. We begin to live in the Presence alone and everything else about it is pure bonus.

Physical love is a psychological-physical impulse. It seeks satisfaction and constant nurturing, like the stoking of a coal stove. It struggles with possessiveness and exults in the kind of ripened openness that enables us to give back as well as to take love wherever, however we can get it. Over time, that kind of love waxes and wanes and, if we're lucky, eventually turns into a bed of embers that never really cools but never really needs as much in the way of stoking to stay real.

Emotional love, that connection to the soul and mind, heart and personality of another is friendship. It is the acme of undying love. It exists without expectations and it grows on air. Unfortunately, it is often confused in a modern world accustomed more to multiple connections than to soul mates. As a result, we talk about "friends" when what we really mean are associates, acquaintances, colleagues, or sometime companions.

A friend, however—a real friend—has grown with us as we have grown. A friend knows our soul, supports us through our weaknesses, prods us, and sustains our strengths. A friend is the person you call at 3:00 a.m. who answers the phone when the pain is unbearable or the fear is destructive. It's a friend who stays on the line with you until all the demons disappear.

It is friendship that sustains and grows the soul through the demands and depths of the spiritual life. Holy friendship is the love that knows us to the core. Sanctifying friendship never dies and never expects to be rewarded for having midwived our best selves to spiritual completeness.

Can anyone live without sex? Of course. Everyone does at some time or other. But no one can live fully—emotionally or

WHAT ARE YOU LOOKING FOR?

spiritually—without a spiritual friend, without human love and understanding.

Metamorphosis, commitment, transformation, and love are the by-products of religious life. If we embrace them wholly and trust them to the end, they can, if we will allow it, take all the parts of our commitment and turn us completely into fire.

No one after lighting a lamp hides it under a jar, or puts it under a bed, but puts it on a lampstand, so that those who enter may see the light (Luke 8:16).

AFTERWORD

To Become a Flame of the Fire

I'm grateful for the opportunity to have been part of this conversation on religious life. It has enabled me to rethink a number of things that I myself have taken for granted in the last fifty years. Was change really a good thing for religious or not? Has it opened up new channels of commitment in the Church or not? Has change energized or depleted religious life?

In a sense, any of those questions can be answered by a simple but certain, "Well, yes…and alternatively, no." It all depends on which dimension of the situation you attend to first. The truth is that all major social change admits of both responses and both responses are true. Some things are gained by change, yes, and at the same time, some things are lost.

Or, to put it another way, to say yes to one thing is always, at the same time, to say no to another. The real value of change depends on what is most needed, most important to the development of the population at the time. Who receives an advantage from the change? Who is being deprived because of it? What good has come from it?

So, as you know, I didn't attempt to answer those questions in this small book. History will be the arbiter of those evaluations.

Instead, and most importantly—at least for you as you work through the throes of your own life decisions—I found myself dealing with three more personal questions instead. First, What gives religious life its energy and its purpose? Second, Is such a life really worthwhile? And third, Does being a religious require us to give up the hope of personal happiness?

1. The fuel of religious life is, pure and simple, the gospel question, "What are you seeking?" If what you are seeking is the magnetizing spirit of Jesus and the role of its message to the world, religious life is a good place to start. If you feel a strong call to one of the gifts Jesus demonstrated to the community, then that gift itself will sustain you for a lifetime.

Like the facets of a diamond, Jesus's gifts—contemplation, courage, justice, community, evangelization, mercy, charity, compassion, peace—are the foundation of one great religious tradition after another. No single religious tradition can give equal light to all of them at the same time. Yet, in each religious tradition one or more gifts emerge more distinctly than the others.

Each religious congregation brings into striking relief a specific aspect of the life of Jesus that must be cultivated if the world itself is to become truly human. If, in fact, the Church itself is to be holy. Jesus's simplicity, for instance, is mirrored by Franciscan poverty. Jesus's evangelizing presence is embedded in the Dominican commitment to pursue truth. Jesus's embrace of all ages and all cultural differences is the foundation of the Benedictine impulse to "receive the visitor as Christ," to make the warmth and care of human community its mark and its goal. Jesus's commitment to justice is defined in the whole of Jesuit history.

Furthermore, every religious congregation that still, as a matter of course, follows the Rules derived from each of those ancient traditions does the same. Jesus the Healer, the Teacher, the Merciful, the Compassionate, the Peacemaker, the Evangelizer, the Just, the Prayerful, the Contemplative shines steadily in one or another of them for all of us to see and emulate.

Therein lies the energy that drives religious life. In the spirit of the Gospels, religious life winds its way from one era to the next, always new, always clear, always courageous. This, of course—this intention to make the Gospels as relevant in our times as they were in all times past—is why religious life never goes away. It never really dies out, though multiple independent congregations may themselves disappear with time, because the gospel is new to every age and must be made newly real there.

2. The second question is an even more specific one: Is religious life worthwhile? In answer to that one, I can only bring the witness of my own more than sixty-five years here. Religious life has been a challenge for me. It often tied me down to the basics when, by personality, I could have been most likely to leap into the off roads of life, wasting both time and energy. At the same time, it gave me a support system that kept pulling me onto greater ideas and questions when I would have loved to simply settle down and bask in an undemanding present.

It brought me to the center of the gospel, where the important questions of life demanded my attention and made more out of me than I might have demanded of myself.

It immersed me daily in the Presence of a present God who has burned away the dross in me and centered me in the essence of life.

For all those things I become more and more grateful every day. But it was not a marshmallow life. It made demands. It spent my strength in ways I never foresaw. It handed me a tradition and made me responsible for it. All those things took courage and built character. The slow way. The hard way. The right way.

But there was a social as well as a personal effect of it on all of us.

In the postwar 1950s, religious life roared into gear, educating a Catholic population that, until at least the mid-1940s, was itself still suspect in a white, Anglo-Saxon, Protestant world.

Our generation saw the last of the great Catholic waves of immigrants—spelled Irish, Italian, Polish, Eastern European. We spilled into a world that, in many cases, was itself actually still fleeing Catholicism and the religious wars that yet lurked in the ashes of the Wars of Religion in Europe. Catholics were not really much wanted here, but religious went on forming Catholic Americans to be good American citizens, nevertheless, because that was the need of the time. Who can understand better than we what it means now to be people of color in a country that defines itself as white? Our task in the world this time is world shaking.

Yes, religious life is still more than worthwhile if we do again for these new Americans what our ancestors did to insert our immigrant families into an equally resistant culture. Religious educated us, fed us, clothed us, housed us, and accompanied us through all the pain that goes with rejection. Now we must do the same for these others, not because they are Catholic but because we are.

As a result, this century's religious congregations have spent the last fifty years creating new service centers where Arabs, Africans, Asians, Hispanics, and others can do the same. Who can say that this kind of gospel presence is not as worthwhile now as it was for us? Who can deny that unity like this is not a sign of the living God?

Clearly, it is making life worthwhile for others that is surely the metric of our own worth.

But the choice of a specific ministry whose purpose is to make the world a better place is also not the only reason that religious life is worthwhile. Pope John Paul II called religious life "the prophetic dimension of the church." And that makes all the difference.

Just as there were bands of prophets in ancient Israel, so are religious communities the institutionalization of prophecy in the Church. The purpose of the religious community is to speak the word of God in its time. It doesn't matter whether anyone listens or not, but it does matter that religious refuse to abandon it. Religious are outside the civic system. They are also outside the official agenda of the Church. But they are bound to speak the missing word of God wherever it is found—in a state or in a church that refuses to address it.

Bartolomé de Las Casas, for instance, a Franciscan friar in the sixteenth century, spoke a prophetic word to the Church in his insistence that Indians have souls and must be treated as equals.

Hildegard of Bingen, a Benedictine nun, spoke a prophetic

word to the Church by refusing to yield her abbatial authority to local clergy and, as a result, she and her community were put under interdict for a year as the entire community refused to yield.

Mary Ward, founder of the Sisters of Loreto, spoke a prophetic word to the Church about the equality of women by appealing to Rome for justice and allowing herself to be exiled rather than surrender her conscience or her new religious community.

Thomas Merton, the Cistercian monk, spoke a prophetic word to Church and state about the universal call to peace in the Christian tradition despite the support of bishops themselves for war.

The religious question is a clear one: Does the Church itself need prophets? Ask women who are challenging the notion that their baptism is inferior to the baptism of males. I'm a woman and I know that only the prophetic word is up to the eradication of sexism.

3. Finally, the third question, whether or not religious life requires that I must give up my own happiness in order to work for the happiness of others, exposes a destructive theological fallacy. Religious life does not exist to prove that "dancing is bad, drinking is bad, hemorrhoids are good."

Suffering, for its own sake, is a distortion of the Christian story. Yes, Jesus suffered but that was not the end of the picture. Jesus rose again in the human heart in a burst of loving glory. For those who have spent life trying with everything in them to make it better for others—to make other people happy, settled, peaceful, secure, competent, respected, and wholly developed—there is no greater personal happiness than to be part of making it happen.

But there is more of value in religious life and community that is beyond the measure of professional achievement, as satisfying as that can be.

There is the joy of spiritual friendship, the companionship of hearts that comes with surviving the pitfalls of the spiritual life— exhaustion when nothing seems to get better, boredom when it all seems the same, depression when it fails, joy when it bursts inside of you with new insight, new depth of soul, and new lifelong commitment to the path.

There is the gift of community, of being known but still accepted—inside and out—with both your strange motives and contorted meanings, despite your erratic indifference as well as your flaming passions and uncommon interests. This lifelong acceptance is the fruit that comes from lifelong personal familiarity and with unfailing communal support, whether we really know ourselves to deserve it or not.

There is the consciousness of growth that takes you beyond your own "smallnesses" to the final and full development of the self.

There is the sense that this is your family, that you are secure in this love, and that, in the end, all will be forgiven.

Indeed, happiness is really what we're all about. What marriage could hope for more?

Finally, it takes courage to turn your back on the three major values of the modern world. It takes courage, barefaced blatant courage, to want something besides money, sex, and power in a country that is built on them. It takes courage to want to be the best of yourself rather than a paper-thin copy of a half-lived life.

But that's what religious life is all about. Religious life is about saying that there is more to life than life empty of substance, life drained of idealism, life lived on a surfeit of trinkets devoid of a spiritual center. It is about spending my life listening to the needs of the world, loving it without exception, and giving every ounce of my very life for it because Jesus, the one we follow, is calling us and has shown the way.

The essayist Leo Rosten says it all, perhaps. "The purpose of life," he writes, "is not to be happy. The purpose of life is to matter, to have it make a difference that you lived at all."

In religious life, we get both: personal happiness and the awareness that we come from a long line of people who, history has made clear, have indeed made a difference.